501 081 668

FOCUS ON TUDOR LIFE

Elizabeth I

Liz Gogerly

Designer Jason Billin
Editor Sarah Ridley
Art Director Jonathan Hair
Editor-in-Chief John C. Miles
Picture research Diana Morris

First published in 2006
by Franklin Watts
338 Euston Road
London NW1 3BH

Franklin Watts Australia
Hachette Children's Books
Level 17/207 Kent Street
Sydney NSW 2000

ISBN 0 7496 6449 5

A CIP catalogue record for this book
is available from the British Library.

Printed in China

Dewey classification number: 942.05'2'092

Note to parents and teachers:
Every effort has been made by the Publishers to ensure that the websites in this book are suitable for children, that they are of the highest educational value, and that they contain no inappropriate or offensive material. However, because of the nature of the Internet, it is impossible to guarantee that the contents of these sites will not be altered. We strongly advise that Internet access is supervised by a responsible adult.

Picture credits
The Royal Collection © 2005 Her Majesty Queen Elizabeth II: front cover, 1, 6

John Bethell/Bridgeman Art Library: 18
T. Alena Brett: 4, 9, 23t, 28
British Library, London/AKG Images: 29t
Sally Chappell/Victoria & Albert Museum, London/Art Archive: 25
Corsham Court, Wilts/Bridgeman Art Library: 27
Eric Crighton/Corbis: 5b
Dagli Orti/Musée du Chateau de Versailles/Art Archive: 13
Mary Evans Picture Library: 11, 20, 29b
HIP/Topfoto: 19b
Erich Lessing/Musée Condé, Chantilly/AKG Images: 5t
Maximillian Collection, Munich/AKG Images: 24
National Portrait Gallery, London/Bridgeman Art Library: 12
Private Collection/Bridgeman Art Library: 26
Private Collection/Philip Mould Historical portraits, London/Bridgeman Art Library: 14
Picturepoint/Topfoto: 7
Roger-Viollet/Topfoto: 23b
Royal Cornwall Museum, Truro/Bridgeman Art Library: 17t
Scottish National Portrait Gallery, Edinburgh/Bridgeman Art Library: 22
Times Newspapers/Rex Features: 21
Victoria & Albert Museum, London/Bridgeman Art Library: 17b
Mike Williams/National Trust Picture Library: 19t.

Every attempt has been made to clear copyright. Should there be any inadvertent omission please apply to the publisher for rectification.

Contents

The Lady Princess

On Sunday, 7 September 1533 Princess Elizabeth was born at Greenwich Palace, near London.

She had pale skin and looked like her father, Henry VIII. Everybody said that her dark eyes were just like those of her mother, Anne Boleyn. Henry was terribly disappointed at the birth of a girl. He had longed for a boy, an heir who would become king after his death.

Henry VIII already had one daughter, Mary, born from his twenty-year marriage to Catherine of Aragon. When Henry met and fell in love with Anne Boleyn, he hoped that she would give him a son and heir. However, to make Anne his queen, he needed to divorce his wife Catherine.

The break with Rome

In those days divorce was out of the question for a monarch. Most people in England belonged to the Roman Catholic Church. The head of this church, also called the Church of Rome, was the Pope. Henry asked Pope Clement VII for his permission to divorce Catherine and was furious when his request was refused. Determined to have his way, he declared himself head of the Church of England, breaking away from the Church of Rome. Then he announced an end to his marriage to Catherine and married Anne. This break with the Roman Catholic Church would cause years of religious unrest.

Henry VIII

Early years

Elizabeth, known as "The Lady Princess", spent her early years at Hatfield House (see panel below) where she rarely saw her parents. Her father, Henry, in time grew tired of her mother and fell in love with another woman, Jane Seymour. Eventually, when Elizabeth was only two years old, Anne was accused of adultery and beheaded. We do not know how this affected Elizabeth because she never spoke or wrote about this dreadful event.

Anne Boleyn. Henry VIII grew tired of her fiery personality.

Elizabeth spent most of her young life in the Old Palace and gardens of Hatfield House.

Go and visit

Hatfield House is about 32 kilometres north of London. The house is surrounded by parkland and woods filled with deer and other game. Elizabeth loved the peace and tranquility at Hatfield. She also developed a lifelong passion for hunting there. The house became her own when she was just 16.

Lady Elizabeth

In May 1536 Henry married Jane Seymour. In many ways Elizabeth's life went on much as before, although now she wasn't known as the Lady Princess.

Instead she was just Lady Elizabeth. Despite the dramatic events going on around her, Elizabeth was becoming a bright and charming little girl. She was thriving under the care of Lady Bryan, the woman who acted as her nanny.

In October 1537 Jane Seymour gave birth to a son called Edward. At last Henry had a male heir. His delight was short-lived because Jane died a couple of weeks later. Lady Bryan was now made Edward's nanny and Elizabeth became the responsibility of Catherine Champernon. Catherine was well-educated and helped Elizabeth with her studies.

Portrait of Elizabeth, aged about 13.

The weaker sex

In Tudor times most people believed that women were not as intelligent as men. They thought that women had fewer morals and were physically weaker too. Elizabeth was unusual because she received the same education as a man. Even so, she once said: "I know that I have the body of a weak and feeble woman, but I have the heart and stomach of a king..."

Elizabeth's brother Edward VI, whom she adored.

A brilliant mind

Elizabeth loved her half-brother Edward. They shared lessons together at Hatfield House where they were taught by some famous scholars of the day. Elizabeth had an amazing memory, excelled at languages and ploughed through books of history and philosophy. Many people commented on her brilliant mind.

Pastimes

As well as being clever, Elizabeth was high-spirited and good fun. She enjoyed dancing, playing musical instruments and hunting. She loved her father dearly but she rarely saw him. On one occasion, in 1542, Henry dined with his daughters, Mary and Elizabeth. He was so impressed with his girls, particularly Elizabeth, that he made sure they were placed in succession to the throne, after Edward.

Elizabeth had four stepmothers but it was Henry's sixth wife, Catherine Parr, who made the biggest impression on her. Elizabeth took a great interest in the religious meetings that Catherine held at court each day.

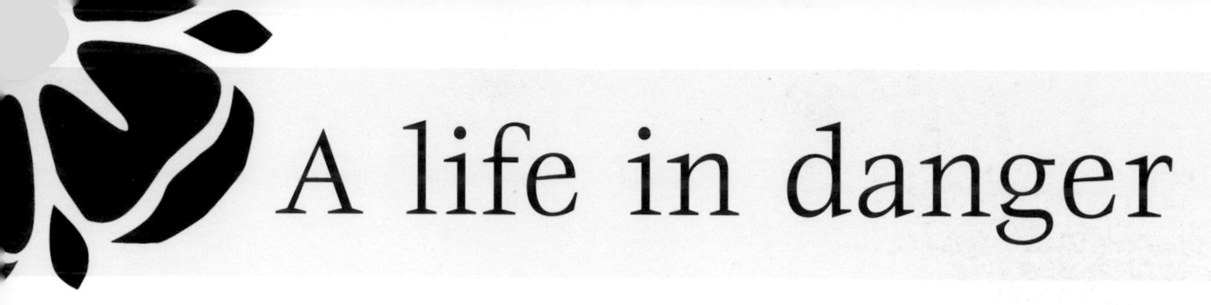

A life in danger

Henry VIII died in 1547. Elizabeth helped to comfort her ten-year-old brother who would soon be crowned Edward VI of England.

Edward was bright but he was terribly young. His uncle, Edward Seymour, helped him to govern the country. During Edward's short reign changes to the Church of England continued. When Edward died suddenly at the age of 16, in 1553, his sister Mary was crowned Queen. Now Elizabeth was next in line to the throne.

A threat to Elizabeth

Mary Tudor was a devout Roman Catholic and was determined to make England wholly Roman Catholic again. She reversed many of the changes made during Henry VIII and Edward VI's reigns. Mary believed that Elizabeth was secretly a Protestant and therefore a threat to her. Many people wanted to depose Mary and put Elizabeth on the throne instead. In fear, Elizabeth distanced herself from her sister and kept away from court.

Roman Catholics and Anglicans

In Tudor times people took religion very seriously. All over Europe, people argued about the right way to worship God. Roman Catholics continued to follow the teachings of the Pope in Rome, attending mass in Latin every Sunday. The Church of England, created when Henry VIII broke away from the Pope's leadership, continued to develop during the sixteenth century. Protestant services were held in English rather than Latin and were simpler in form. More emphasis was placed on the word of God as revealed through the Bible, rather than through rituals and sacraments such as holy communion.

Queen Mary, who imprisoned Elizabeth in the Tower of London.

The Wyatt Rebellion

By now Mary was desperate to marry and produce a Catholic heir. In 1554 she looked set to marry King Philip II of Spain. Many people didn't like Philip and decided it was time to act against Mary. Sir Thomas Wyatt and his followers hatched a plot to get rid of her but it failed and the plotters were executed. Mary was convinced that Elizabeth was connected to the plot. She ordered her sister to be arrested and kept in the Tower of London for nearly three months. Each day that passed Elizabeth believed was her last. When she was eventually released, without charge, she believed that it was God's will.

Long live the Queen

Mary Tudor married Philip II of Spain in 1555 but died, childless, in 1558. Elizabeth was declared her successor.

Elizabeth was in the park at Hatfield when she heard the news. As she was presented with Mary's coronation ring Elizabeth knelt down and declared in Latin: "God has done it and it is marvellous in our eyes!" By now Elizabeth was 25 years old, tall, slender and with the look of a queen.

A few days later Elizabeth appeared before her new Privy Council in the Great Hall at Hatfield (right). She spoke confidently as she made her first formal address: "I mean to direct all mine actions by good advice and counsel. My meaning is to require of you all nothing more but faithful hearts, and of my good will you shall not doubt, using yourselves as good and loving subjects."

Cecil and Dudley

Many of those present were impressed, including Sir William Cecil who Elizabeth had appointed her Principal Secretary of State. He would be her loyal adviser for the next forty years. Also in attendance was Robert Dudley, one of Elizabeth's closest and most trusted friends.

Elizabeth arrived in London a couple of days later, part of a procession of over a thousand nobles, gentlemen and women, riding on horseback. People cheered as she passed by and it seemed Elizabeth had already won the hearts of many of her people.

She who must be obeyed

Elizabeth always maintained high standards at her court. She refused to employ anybody who was ugly – a young man was once denied employment because he had a front tooth missing.

Elizabeth hated being disobeyed. Her ladies-in-waiting were expected to ask her permission before they married. Nobody was allowed to sit while she stood, and anyone addressing the Queen had to do so on bended knee.

The Great Hall at Hatfield House

A magnificent coronation

Elizabeth was crowned queen at a magnificent coronation ceremony on 15 January 1559.

Even though England was not a rich country, Elizabeth insisted that her coronation appear grand and extravagant. She wanted to show people that she was the rightful heir to the throne. Most of all she wanted to mark the beginning of a new age.

Long Live the Queen!
Celebrations began on the eve of the coronation. Elizabeth believed she should be seen by her people and was paraded through the streets on a litter that was open on every side. Many people adored her already and applauded her as she passed by. Elizabeth stopped to give kind words to the elderly and poor and accept little posies of flowers from the children.

A portrait of Elizabeth in the state robe for her coronation, including a mantle (cloak) trimmed with ermine fur. She holds the orb (right) and sceptre.

A great day

The next day Elizabeth was crowned in Westminster Abbey. She was anointed with holy oil, the crown was placed on her head and she was handed the orb and sceptre – symbols of the monarch's power. Parts of the coronation service was conducted in Latin for the last time in British history, but other parts of the service were in English. Later, there was a banquet at Westminster Hall that lasted for ten hours.

When the celebrations finally ended Elizabeth was exhausted but overjoyed to be Queen of England.

Dressed to impress

Elizabeth believed that how she looked was important. Her clothes and jewels were carefully chosen to make her stand out. Often it took two hours to get her dressed. Many of her dresses were finely embroidered with flowers and insects. As Elizabeth grew older her taste in clothes became even more extravagant and full of meaning. In the Rainbow Portrait of 1600 (above) her clothes are decorated with eyes and ears to symbolise her fame.

The Queen means business

Elizabeth was eager to get down to the serious business of ruling the country.

The opening of Parliament took place on 25 January 1559 and the new queen immediately made her mark. Even though she was a woman, Elizabeth said she would not be told what to do. She made it clear that, as an absolute monarch, she had total power over the country.

Ruling the country

Throughout her reign Elizabeth enjoyed being in control but she was wise enough to listen to the advice given by her Privy Council. Each day she set a time for official matters and met with William Cecil. Even though she was fond of music, dance and lively conversation, it is said that she always enjoyed matters of government even more. This was important because she had many problems, including a country that was bitterly divided over religion.

Head of the Church

Elizabeth was keen to reform the Church but she did not want to make enemies of the Roman Catholic Church. In matters of religion she aimed to take "a middle way". In May 1559 the Church of England became established by law. Now those who refused to attend church on Sunday could be fined. Elizabeth herself became Supreme Governor of the Church.

Money worries

Elizabeth had inherited debts from her father and sister. During her reign she managed to pay back this money. She did this by raising taxes, selling off land owned by the Crown and living on a tight budget. She spent money on the things she considered important. Her palaces looked magnificent but she only made necessary alterations and repairs to the buildings. Many of her staff received no wage increases.

The young queen – a portrait painted in the early 1560s.

Who will be King?

"I will never marry!"

Elizabeth was a teenager when she said this. As reigning Queen, she was under enormous pressure to find a husband and have children. At that time most people didn't think a woman could rule a country alone. There was also the question of Elizabeth's successor. The answer was to marry and have children. When the issue was raised in Parliament Elizabeth was annoyed and said:

"I am already bound unto a husband, which is the kingdom of England."

Who next?

Elizabeth did not like discussing who would succeed her to the throne and throughout her reign kept everyone guessing on this issue. Possible contenders were Lady Katherine and Lady Mary Grey. Many Roman Catholics believed that Elizabeth's cousin, the Catholic Mary Stuart, who became Mary Queen of Scots, was the rightful Queen of England. By English law this was not so, but nevertheless Elizabeth was always wary of her cousin.

Marriage offers

During the first months of her reign Elizabeth received a number of marriage proposals. First came the offer from her brother-in-law, Philip II of Spain. Elizabeth considered her position carefully but eventually told Philip that she did not wish to marry at all.

Meanwhile, the Holy Roman Emperor, Ferdinand I, believed Elizabeth might be a good match for one of his sons. Again, she kept the Emperor waiting for an answer. Then Erik of Sweden asked for her hand in marriage.

A royal picnic. Elizabeth and Robert Dudley enjoy music in the open air.

Elizabeth's favourite, Robert Dudley. She admired his hunting, dancing and jousting skills.

Robert Dudley

Elizabeth was enjoying all this attention but she was also becoming closer to Robert Dudley, whom she made Earl of Leicester. It was rumoured that if he were free of his wife they would marry. Dudley's wife died in 1560 but some people thought Dudley had her murdered. Now Elizabeth could never marry him.

In the end, perhaps Elizabeth loved power too much to share it with anyone. Over the years she had many suitors but she turned them all down.

England's splendid houses

When she succeeded the throne, Elizabeth inherited about 60 royal palaces and houses.

Most of the palaces were by the River Thames, in and around London. Whitehall Palace was in the centre of London. It had over 2,000 rooms and it was Elizabeth's main residence in the winter. Richmond Palace lay west of London and Elizabeth enjoyed spending some of the cold winter months there. Further west lay Hampton Court, a magnificent palace with 800 rooms. One of Elizabeth's favourite places was Nonsuch in Surrey, a romantic-looking palace built by her father.

The entrance to Hampton Court Palace

On tour

Most summers Elizabeth went on a grand tour of her royal palaces and the homes of her courtiers. Usually, she travelled in an open carriage so that ordinary people could see her. Whenever she returned to London it was a magnificent occasion. Elizabeth rode into the city with streams of courtiers on horses behind her.

Hardwick Hall in Derbyshire

Home improvements

Elizabeth loved to be entertained by her courtiers. During her reign many beautiful country houses were built or improved for her visits. William Cecil, who became Lord Burghley, built special chambers and created gardens for the Queen at his home, Burghley House. Another famous house from Elizabethan times was Hardwick Hall. Its owner, the Dowager Countess of Shrewsbury, or Bess of Hardwick, hoped that Elizabeth might visit the grand new house she'd built. Despite Bess's great efforts, the Queen never visited Hardwick Hall.

Go and visit

Elizabeth gave Kenilworth Castle in Warwickshire - now a ruin - to Robert Dudley in 1563. He immediately set about making it into one of the grandest homes in England. Elizabeth visited there many times but it was her stay in 1575 which was most remembered. She stayed for ten days and was treated to torch-lit dinners, music and fireworks. It is said that when Elizabeth told Dudley that she couldn't see the new gardens from her bedroom he had a garden built overnight under the Queen's window.

Life at the Royal Court

In Tudor times the Royal Court moved with the monarch.

At times there could be as many as 15,000 people in attendance on Elizabeth. Life at the Royal Court was exciting but it was competitive too as people tried to outdo each other to gain the Queen's favour. Elizabeth was most impressed by good manners, lively wit and intelligence. She also favoured the great explorers of the day, who risked their lives to make England great. Francis Drake was a favourite who brought back many treasures from his travels and shared them with Elizabeth.

Elizabeth's court has been described as a stage where she could show off her riches to visiting foreign ambassadors and statesmen. Her banquets were lavish and often followed by dancing or tournaments. Elizabeth also supported the great musicians of her time.

Poetry for the Queen

Poets were also welcomed into court. In 1589 the poet Edmund Spenser went to London to lay his epic poem *The Faerie Queen* at the feet of the Queen. By now Elizabeth promoted herself as the Virgin Queen – a woman married to her country. In his poem Spenser called her "Gloriana", a title which no doubt delighted the Queen.

While much of court life was about being seen, the Queen kept some time for herself. She usually stayed up late at night so she slept late in the mornings. Then she would dress and take a walk before breakfast.

Jonson, Shakespeare and the theatre

The court became famous for promoting the theatre. Plays by William Shakespeare and Ben Jonson were performed before the Queen. The Globe Theatre in London opened in 1599. Elizabeth's love of plays helped to make it popular. Shakespeare is believed to have written *The Merry Wives of Windsor* and *Twelfth Night* especially for her. But Elizabeth liked to laugh as well and enjoyed the antics of court jesters, the comedians of the day.

Shakespeare's Globe Theatre has been recreated close to its original site in London, and you can visit it.

Plots against the Queen

Mary Queen of Scots had lived in France since she was a girl and in 1558 married King Francis II of France.

Elizabeth never trusted her Roman Catholic cousin, but when Mary returned to Scotland after the death of Francis II, Elizabeth became even more wary.

For a few years Mary was popular in Scotland but a disastrous marriage to Henry, Lord Darnley put her out of favour. In 1566 she gave birth to a son, James, the heir to the Scottish throne. In 1567 Darnley was murdered and a few months later Mary married the Earl of Bothwell, the man believed to have killed Darnley. Now Mary was forced to give up her throne. Her enemies captured and imprisoned her. In 1568 she escaped and fled to England where she asked for Elizabeth's help.

This medal commemorates the marriage of Mary Queen of Scots and Henry, Lord Darnley.

The Northern Rebellion

Elizabeth had little choice but to keep Mary locked up for the next 19 years. During that time she became the centre of many plots to get rid of Elizabeth. The first serious attempt to overthrow Elizabeth was the Northern Rebellion, a Catholic uprising in northern England in 1569. The threat was most alarming because France and Spain supported the rebels. The plot failed.

In 1570 Pope Pius V excommunicated Elizabeth. More Catholic plots followed, including the Ridolfi Plot of 1571 in which the Duke of Norfolk attempted to free Mary. In 1572 Norfolk was executed but Elizabeth refused to have Mary killed due to lack of proof. The number of plots against her forced Elizabeth to take a much more hardline approach to Roman Catholics as her reign progressed, resulting in many priests and ordinary Catholics being executed for treason.

Mary Queen of Scots

Execution of Mary

It was many years later, in 1585, that Mary was finally caught plotting against Elizabeth. The Babington Plot was serious because Philip II of Spain supported it. Elizabeth did not want her cousin to be executed but Parliament convinced her there was no other way. On 8 February 1587 Mary Queen of Scots was beheaded.

The royal spymaster

Brilliant and ruthless, Sir Francis Walsingham was a man in whom Elizabeth had utter faith and trust. Walsingham acted as Secretary of State and placed about 50 undercover agents in the royal courts of Europe. He strongly disliked both Spain and Mary Queen of Scots. It was Walsingham's spies who revealed the Babington Plot of 1585. A few years later they supplied important information about the Spanish Armada.

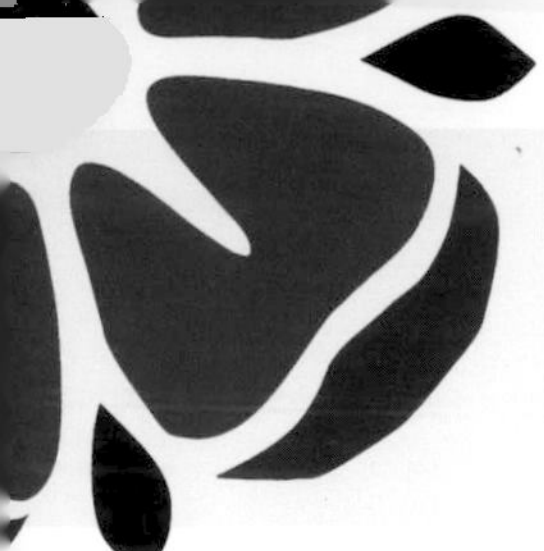

Elizabeth at war

Throughout her reign Elizabeth tried to avoid war but sometimes she acted to weaken other countries.

After the Northern Rebellion of 1569 the threat of a Spanish attack on England became more real. At this time Philip II controlled parts of the Netherlands. Elizabeth sent English troops to help Dutch rebels fight their Spanish masters. She also secretly supported Protestants in France rebelling against the Catholic king.

This painting shows Elizabeth visiting troops at Tilbury in 1588. She gave a famous speech:

"I am come amongst you not for my recreation and disport, but being resolved in the midst and heat of the battle to live or die amongst you all, to lay down for my God and my kingdom, and for my people, my honour and my blood, even in dust."

Rivalry with Spain

Spain was a powerful nation with colonies in the New World. Elizabeth saw her chance to weaken the Spanish there and to increase her own country's wealth. She sent English sailors, like Sir Francis Drake, to steal treasure from Spanish ships. This made Philip II furious.

The Armada

The execution of Mary Queen of Scots and the worsening treatment of Roman Catholics in England forced Philip to take action against Elizabeth. In the summer of 1588 he launched a fleet of 130 Spanish ships, carrying 30,000 men and 2,500 guns. The fleet was called the Armada and the plan was to invade England, place Philip II's daughter on the throne and make England a Roman Catholic country once more.

Elizabeth was ready for war. An army of about 20,000 men had gathered at Tilbury and a fleet of 150 ships waited at Plymouth. On 9 August Elizabeth visited the troops at Tilbury and gave a powerful speech (see panel opposite). By now the English navy had begun fighting the Armada. Helped by great storms that scattered the Spanish ships, the English were able to defeat the mighty Armada. Elizabeth was triumphant!

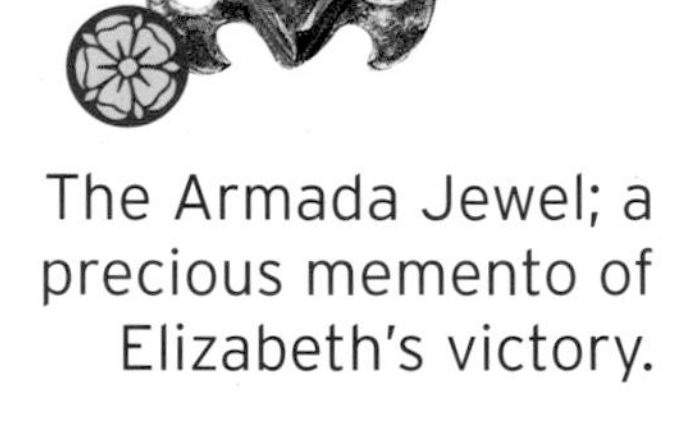

The Armada Jewel; a precious memento of Elizabeth's victory.

The end of the affair

Elizabeth's happiness after defeating the Armada was short-lived. Robert Dudley, Earl of Leicester, died on 4 September 1588. He had been at Elizabeth's side at Tilbury but had fallen ill a few weeks later. Elizabeth was grief-sticken to have lost the man she called "her brother and best friend". She kept his last letter to her by her bedside, where it was found when she died many years later.

High days and dark days

Victory over the Armada turned Elizabeth into one of the most powerful monarchs of her time.

Even the Pope was impressed: "She is only a woman ... and yet she makes herself feared by Spain, by France, by the Empire, by all!" By defeating the Spanish, Elizabeth also brought more stability at home. Roman Catholics and Protestants were united in their respect for their Queen and the Church of England became stronger.

By now Elizabeth was fifty-five years old. She was still fit and healthy but the death of Robert Dudley had been a terrible blow. In the following years many of her advisers also died.

Elizabeth's courtiers carry her in the royal litter at the wedding ceremony of Lord Herbert in June 1600. The bride, Anne Russell, stands just behind the litter in her white dress.

Royal decline

Elizabeth didn't like being ill and often refused to take medicine or see a doctor. In the 1560s she nearly died when she caught smallpox.

As she grew older she suffered from terrible toothache but flatly refused to have her teeth pulled out. Towards the end of her life her eyes began to fail and she lost her memory. For Tudor times, however, Elizabeth was considered a very fit old woman.

Elizabeth in her later years. The figures behind her represent Time (left) and Death.

Elizabeth and Essex

In his final years, William Cecil had groomed his son Robert to take over his responsibilities. The Queen trusted Robert but there were more exciting faces at court. Robert Devereux, Earl of Essex, was the stepson of Robert Dudley and quickly became the Queen's favourite. For a while they did everything together and she gave him political power. But eventually, Essex's thirst for power led him to rebel against the Queen, for which he was executed in 1601.

Problems of the 1590s

Elizabeth's final years were beset with other problems. The threat of a Spanish invasion never went away and Elizabeth spent more money on defence. Taxes went up and in parts of the country there were riots. Then in the 1590s there was a series of failed harvests that caused soaring food prices and starvation for many.

End of an era

After Essex's execution the Queen seemed sad and had less time for the business of government.

In the later years of Elizabeth's reign Parliament had grown more powerful. There was also more unrest on the streets of England. People began to question whether Elizabeth was too old to deal with problems such as rising taxes, the increase in the number of beggars or the war with Spain. Some people even wished that Essex had succeeded in his rebellion against the Queen.

In November 1601 Elizabeth spoke before Parliament. Near the end of the speech she told them:
"There will never Queen sit in my seat with more zeal to my country, care to my subjects, and that will sooner with willingness venture her life for your good and safety than myself."

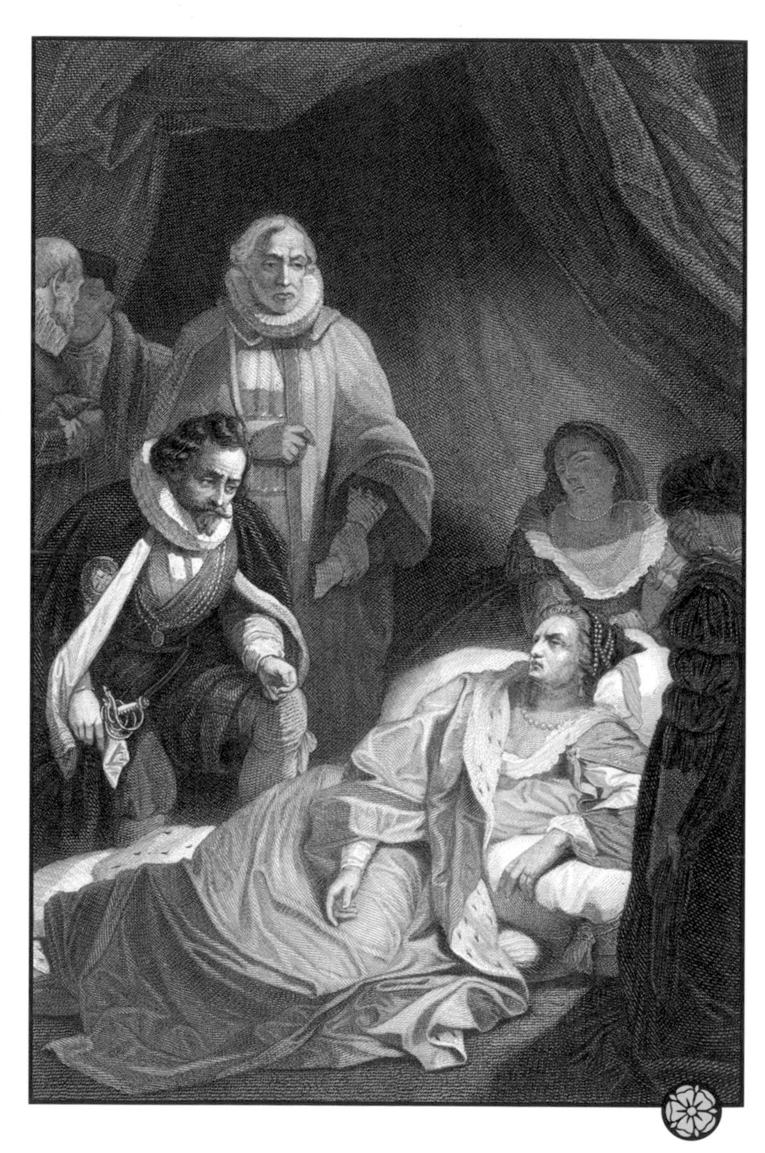

A 19th century impression of Elizabeth's death at Richmond Palace.

Last speech to Parliament

A few weeks later Elizabeth made her final appearance in Parliament. In her speech she summed up the major events of her reign but she didn't say who would succeed the throne. In recent years she had been writing to James VI of Scotland, the son of Mary Queen of Scots. Even so, she didn't name him as her successor.

Elizabeth's funeral procession makes its way to Westminster Abbey.

Naming a successor

In 1602 Elizabeth was in good health but early the next year she seemed to tire of life. When she caught a fever in March 1603, Robert Cecil begged her to name her successor. At the end she could barely speak but made it known that James VI of Scotland was her choice. Elizabeth I died on 24 March 1603.

After her burial at Westminster Abbey, Elizabeth seemed to regain the popularity she had lost in recent years. She was remembered as a Queen who brought peace and prosperity to England and became known as "Good Queen Bess".

Go and visit

Elizabeth is buried in the beautiful Henry VII Chapel at Westminster Abbey. She was never close to her sister Mary Tudor but they share the same tomb. On the other side of the chapel lies Elizabeth's cousin, Mary Queen of Scots. At the Abbey Treasure Museum you can see the ring that Elizabeth gave to Robert Devereux, Earl of Essex.

GLOSSARY

ambassador
A person sent to a foreign country on official business.

banquet
A meal for a large number of people to celebrate a special occasion.

clergy
Priests in the Christian church.

courtier
A person who attends the Royal Court.

devout
Deeply religious.

excommunicate
To exclude a person from the Roman Catholic Church.

fanfare
A sounding of trumpets or bugles on a special occasion.

formal address
A specially prepared speech for an official occasion.

heir
Someone who will be given money, property or a title when somebody else dies.

holy day
A religious festival.

inherit
To get money, property or a title from somebody who has died.

jester
An entertainer at the Royal Court.

kinsmen
People related to you.

lady-in-waiting
A lady companion to a queen or princess.

litter
A small platform with a chair or sofa that can be carried on men's shoulders.

modified
Changed slightly.

monarch
A King or Queen.

morals
The ability to know what is right and wrong.

New World
North and South America.

ornate
Highly decorated.

Privy Council
The advisers appointed by a monarch.

Protestant Church
A new branch of the Christian Church that was set up in Tudor times, rejecting the rule of the Pope.

ruff
A stiff frill worn around the neck.

Secretary of State
The head of a major government department.

statesman
A person involved in the political affairs of a country.

successor
The person who will take over a position from somebody else.

suitor
A man who wants to marry a particular woman.

tournament
A pageant where knights compete against each other in different events, such as jousting.

treason
The crime of betraying your country or plotting against the King or Queen.

TIMELINE

7 September 1533: Elizabeth is born at Greenwich Palace, London.

9 May 1536: Anne Boleyn is executed.

January 1547: Henry VIII dies.

6 July 1553: Edward VI dies and is succeeded by Mary I.

17 November 1558: Mary I dies and is succeeded by Elizabeth.

15 January 1559: Elizabeth's coronation ceremony.

1561: Francis II of France dies, and Mary Queen of Scots returns to Scotland.

1568: Mary Queen of Scots flees to England and is imprisoned by Elizabeth.

1570: Elizabeth is excommunicated by Pope Pius V.

1571: Ridolfi Plot to overthrow Elizabeth is discovered.

1571: Elizabeth names William Cecil Lord Treasurer and gives him the new title of Lord Burleigh. Francis Walsingham replaces him as Secretary of State.

1575: Robert Dudley entertains Elizabeth at Kenilworth Castle.

1577–1580 Francis Drake sails around the world in *The Golden Hind*.

1580: Pope Gregory XIII announces that killing Elizabeth is not a sin.

1586: Babington Plot to overthrow Elizabeth is uncovered.

8 February 1587: Mary Queen of Scots is executed.

1588: Launch and defeat of Philip II of Spain's Armada.

1588: Robert Dudley dies.

1590: Sir Francis Walsingham dies.

1598: Lord Burghley (William Cecil) dies.

25 February 1601: Robert Devereux, Earl of Essex, is executed for treason.

24 March 1603: Queen Elizabeth I dies and is succeeded by James VI of Scotland who becomes James I of England.

PLACES TO VISIT

Burghley House, Stamford, Lincolnshire
The home of William Cecil, Lord Burghley.

Fotheringhay Castle, Peterborough, Northamptonshire
The site of Mary Queen of Scots execution.

Hardwick Hall, near Chesterfield, Derbyshire
The home of Bess of Hardwick.

Hatfield House, Hatfield, Hertfordshire
The childhood home of Elizabeth I.

Kenilworth Castle, Kenilworth, Warwickshire
The home of Robert Dudley, Earl of Leicester. Though now a ruin, you can still visit the beautiful gardens.

Loch Leven Castle, Loch Leven, Scotland
Visit the castle where Mary Queen of Scots was imprisoned. It's in the middle of the loch (lake) so you'll be taken there by boat!

Tower of London, Tower Hill, London
Elizabeth was imprisoned here for three months.

Westminster Abbey, London
Elizabeth's final resting place.

WEBSITES

http://tudorhistory.org/elizabeth/
An interesting biography of Elizabeth I with lots of contemporary paintings.

http://www.historylearningsite.co.uk/elizabeth_i.htm
A good place to learn about Elizabeth and all the other Tudor monarchs.

www.bbc.co.uk/history/state/monarchs_leaders/elizabeth_i_01.shtml
A site with timelines and information about the major historic events during Elizabeth's reign.

http://tudors.crispen.org/tudor_women/index.html
Find out what it was like being a woman during the Tudor age.

http://www.snaithprimary.eril.net/ttss.htm
A lively site prepared especially for school children. Lots of interesting activities.

http://www.tudorbritain.org/
A fabulous site for children learning about Elizabeth and the Tudors. Created by the Victoria and Albert Museum.

INDEX